PERMISSION
to
LAND

Personal Transformation
Through Writing

Writing transforms the soul! Marci Brockmann

MARCI BROCKMANN

Permission to Land: Personal Transformation Through Writing
The Full Self-Paced Course
is a work of non-fiction.

Copyright 2020 by Marci Brockmann.

Published in the United States by Marci Brockmann.

LIBRARY OF CONGRESS CATALOGING-IN-PUBLICATION DATA

NAMES: Brockmann, Marci, author.

TITLE: Permission to Land:
Personal Transformation Through Writing
The Full Self-Paced Course
by
Marci Brockmann

IDENTIFIERS:
ISBN Paperback: 978-1-64746-339-7

SUBJECTS: 1. Brockmann, Marci. 2. Journal–Diary–Guided Journal
3. Expressive Writing–Writing Prompts.
4. Self-Help 5. Personal Education
6. Life Analysis 7. Self-Awareness—Personal Growth—Journaling.
8. Love—Relationships–Romance
9. Marriage—Remarriage. 10. Mental Health 11. Title—
Permission to Land:
Personal Transformation Through Writing – The Full Self-Paced Course

Printed in the United States.
Book Design by Debbie O'Byrne

"Owning a story and loving ourselves through that process is the bravest thing that we will ever do."—Brené Brown.

"Even when it's not pretty or perfect. Even when it's more real than you want it to be. Your story is what you have, what you will always have. It is something to own."—Michelle Obama

"Journaling is like whispering to one's self and listening at the same time."—Bram Stoker, Dracula

"People change and things go wrong but just remember life goes on."—Mac Miller

Permission to Land:
Transformation Through Writing

"The years go by. The time, it does fly.
Every single second is a moment in time that passes.
And it seems like nothing—but when you're looking back...
well, it amounts to everything."—Ray Bradbury

Permission to Land: Transformation Through Writing is a self-directed course in writing your own story for personal memory, discovery, and growth.

I invite you to take a personal journey to excavate your own path, dig out memories and phantoms from your own brain, see how you can fit the pieces together and take the long view back of your own life. Journaling with this self-paced course, which is a companion to *Permission to Land: Searching for Love, Home & Belonging*, will be thought provoking and introspective as there are over 100 pages of inspiring writing prompts to trigger memories and give you the space in which to create your own written narrative of your life. It is a genuinely cathartic experience that will set you free, at least in some respect and to some degree.

Expressive writing helps banish the demons that haunt you and encourages the memories to bloom. Write the joy, laughter, and the love. Set it all free into the universe, where it can all mingle and part the heavens. And in so doing, you will lighten your heart and free it from worry and the burden of carrying all those memories around. Who wouldn't want a lighter load to carry?

Setting aside regular time for expressive writing is so vital to inner peace as it is one of the greatest methods of processing emotions and situational experiences. Set an alarm or a calendar reminder for yourself to help you set aside the time to write. (I have an alarm that rings every day at 4pm.) When we write what is in our hearts, we see what we have written, we allow what has been bottled up to breathe outside of our minds and hearts and, in doing so, we gain a little distance from them, gain a clearer perspective and a deeper sense of understanding of ourselves.

Writing can increase someone's acceptance of their experience, and acceptance is calming. We are all much deeper and much more hidden than we probably would be comfortable admitting and this process can open your heart and soul. In these pages, you have the freedom to explore your own memories and experiences and put yourself on a healthy path toward the life of your dreams, more clearly define who you are, where you have been and where you want to go. What a gift that is!

What else will you get out of it? Catharsis. Understanding. Memory. Growth. Healing. Priceless!

This is your story. Start your journey now.
I'll walk with you hand-in-hand as you get there.
Happy writing!

How would I describe myself in 15 words?

My favorite way to spend the
day is…

What do I love about my life right now?

As a child, what were my dreams?

How have my dreams evolved throughout my life?

Where did I grow up? What was my childhood like?

My favorite memory of my childhood is...

Of what am I (or was I) the most afraid? What does (or did) that feel like?

What does unconditional love
mean to me? What does it feel
like? With whom have I shared this
kind of love?

Who are/were my parents? What are/were they like? What do/did they do for a living?

How did my parents'
personalities and habits
influence me to become who I am?

_____

_____

_____

_____

_____

_____

_____

_____

_____

_____

_____

_____

_____

_____

_____

_____

_____

_____

_____

When I think of my parents, how do I feel?

What did the home and room I
lived in as a child look like? Did
I feel safe there?

Who are my siblings and earliest friends? What impact do they have on my life?

How has my relationship with my siblings (and other family members) changed over the years?

What does friendship mean to me and how has that evolved through my life?

Who are/were my grandparents? What were or are they like?

How does/did having or not having them in my life make me feel?

_____

_____

_____

_____

_____

_____

_____

_____

_____

_____

_____

_____

_____

_____

_____

_____

_____

_____

_____

_____

_____

What traditions have been passed down through the generations of my family? What feelings to they evoke?

What family traditions are important to share with my present or future children?

What are my memories of school and my education?

Who were my most memorable teachers and how did they help me change or evolve?

What role did sports, music or other extra-curricular activities have in my childhood/adolescence?

If I could talk to my teenage
self, the one piece of advice I
would give is...

If I could change one thing about my younger self what would that be?

How do I deal with conflict?
How do I deal with differences
of opinion with friends? Family?
Co-Workers?

What were my first romantic and/or sexual experiences? How did they shape my beliefs about myself?

As I grew up, what were my goals for the future? How did they evolve over time?

Who was my first love? How did we meet? How long were we together? What are my most vivid memories of that relationship?

Is there a perfect life?
Why do we strive for perfection
if it is not attainable?

How has love, romance and
sex influenced my choices and
decisions?

Describe the most significant relationships of my life. What makes them significant? What do/did they teach me about myself?

Would I forgive my spouse or significant other for infidelity?

What are my views of family?
(My family of origin as well as
any I have chosen.)

As I matured, what about me
has changed? What has stayed
constant?

How do I define loyalty? How does it feel when my trust is broken?

What has been the most surprising about my life so far?

What has my career path
been like? How did I decide to
pursue those goals? Does my chosen
path(s) bring meaning to my life?

What experiences with my various jobs bring my life meaning?

How has my current vocation created my self-perception? What do I like the most/least about what I do?

What were my biggest mistakes and what have I learned from them?

This is a list of 30 things that make me smile.

The words I'd like to live
by are...

_____

_____

_____

_____

_____

_____

_____

_____

_____

_____

_____

_____

_____

_____

_____

_____

_____

I really wish others knew this about me...

What surprised me the most about my life or life in general?

Who are my most trusted friends? How has our friendship evolved over time?

These things are guilty pleasures in my life.

These are people in my life who genuinely support me, and who I can genuinely trust. (I need to make time to hang out with them.)

Which have been the five best days of my life? What makes them so memorable?

If I could go back in time to relive, redo, replay, revise any five days in my life what days would they be? (Ignore problems that may be caused by the butterfly effect.)

What words do I need to hear
the most and from whom? How
would it make me feel to hear them?

These experiences are on my
bucket list and I chose them
because...

I believe in....

What are my favorite movies? How have they changed my life?

What are my favorite books?
How have they changed
my life?

What is my favorite music? How has it changed my life?

As I have lived my life so far, I've come to realize what is really and truly important and that is....

I feel most energized when...

My unusual, unexpected or
hidden skill or talent is…

What advice do I think is important to tell my children or younger friends/family?

Of what am I the proudest?

What would I like to talk about with my parents or grandparents if I could without fear of overstepping or hurting their feelings, (or because they are no longer in my life)?

This is a list of all the live music or comedy concerts or live theatre productions I have seen and memories I have of these special times.

Pets/animals are so very
special in our lives. These are
the pets/animals have been very
important in my life.

Before I leave this life, I want to
be sure to...

I don't like to admit this, but...

When I look back across my
lifetime, however long I have
lived, I am least proud of....

The things I regret the most are....

My plan for the next 5 years?
10 years? (or maybe this week.)

How old would I be if I didn't know how old I am?

Which is worse, failing or never trying?

If life is so short, why do we do
so many things we don't like
and like so many things we don't do?

What is the one thing I'd most like to change about the world?

To what degree have I actually controlled the course my life has taken?

What are my views about forgiveness?

Would I break the law to save a loved one? Why?

If I had to move to a state
or country besides the one I
currently live in, where would I move
and why?

What one thing have I not done that I really want to do? What's holding me back?

What am I holding onto that I need to let go of?

Why am I me?

Which is worse, when a good friend moves away, or losing touch with a good friend who lives right near you?

Has my greatest fear ever come true?

How important is what others think of me? How important is my reputation?

Do I remember that time 5 years ago when I was extremely upset? Does it really matter now?

At what time in my
recent past have I felt
most passionate and alive?

If I haven't achieved my biggest dreams yet, why have I not? What do I have to lose?

Is it possible to know, without a doubt, what is good and what is evil?

If I just won five million dollars, would I quit my job?

What is the difference between being alive and truly living?

If I knew that everyone
I know was going to die
tomorrow, who would I visit today?

If we learn from our mistakes,
why are we always so afraid to
make them?

What would I do differently if I knew nobody would judge me?

What would I do differently if I knew I would not judge myself?

Five years from now will I
remember what I did yesterday?
What about the day before that? Or
the day before that?

Why do we dream? Describe a dream I have had.

Is it possible to live a normal life and not ever tell a lie?

If I could become immortal
on the condition that I would
NEVER be able to die or kill myself,
would I choose immortality?
Why or why not?

What actions in my life will
have the longest reaching
consequences? How long will those
effects be felt?

Is there a meaning to life? If so, what is it?

Would I confess to something I didn't do if it meant that it would save my life? The life of a stranger? The life of a friend? The life of a family member?

Where does my self-worth come from?

Morality and ethics define who
a person is. Why do I think this is
or isn't true?

How has my view of myself
changed having taken this long
view back over your life?

As I begin the next phase of my
life, I want to....

When I am really honest with myself....

Now that I've answered all
these questions and taken
a look at my life, my memories,
behaviors, and feelings, what
patterns do I see emerge?

In what ways has completing this self-paced writing course changed the way I see myself?

About the Author

Marci Brockmann has journaled for over forty years and swears it keeps her sane. She is a columnist for the Elephant Journal and an accomplished artist. She earned her B.A. from SUNY New Paltz, an M.A. from LIU/Post and an M.S. from University of Phoenix, and she has been a high school English teacher for more than twenty-five years. She lives in Long Island, NY, with her husband, their kids, frisky cats, and many fishes.

Website: www.MarciBrockmann.com
Facebook: Marci527 & marcibrockmannartist
YouTube Channel: What's up, Marci?
Instagram: @marcibrockmann & @marcibrockmann27
Blog: What's up, Marci? - Whatsupmarci.com
Media Kit: https://tinyurl.com/ybva5nfy

Reviews of Permission to Land:
Searching for Love, Home & Belonging

"Love this book! I have only read 5 chapters, but I have found this to be a wonderful book. Frequently as I am reading, I am finding that I can relate to do much of it. I would highly recommend this book!"
— Ellen W

"This candid and emotionally charged memoir takes us on a captivating journey. We share the author's frustration over her repeated attempts to deal rationally with her once loving and generous mother, who has become mentally ill and drug addicted. We cringe at the resulting abuse Ms. Brockman suffers, and her mother's inability to give her the love she so desperately needs, which negatively impacted the author's self-perception and future relationships. The desire to be loved and the need to belong kept Marci Brockmann striving, and her writing, artwork, and psychotherapy kept her from succumbing to the same fate as her mother, or worse. Permission to Land, with Ms. Brockman's casual and intimate writing style, keeps you turning the pages, and you find yourself caring about her, rooting for her, and respecting her for kind heart, her courage in seeking the help she needed and in facing the pain of her past, her tenacity in pursuing the life she wanted and deserved, her willingness to accept responsibility for her choices, and for her generosity in telling her story and, thereby, instilling hope in us all. I highly recommend this book to anyone who enjoys an engrossing story, anyone who has suffered, anyone who can use a dose of hope, and anyone who wants to create a happier life."
— Sandra D, PhD

"Very enjoyable read. Marci gives inspiration to anybody who wants a life change. No matter what your background - you CAN achieve the life you want. Your childhood experiences do not have to define you. You can choose to be a victim, or you can overcome. Marci clearly has overcome."
— Harry D

Buy art from
living artists
the dead ones don't need the money

---

www.MarciBrockmann.com

Original paintings.   **Custom prints.**   **Gorgeous scarves.**

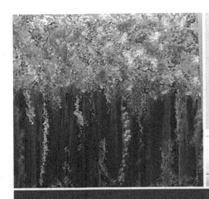

MarciBrockmann.com

ORIGINAL PAINTINGS, CUSTOM PRINTS, SILKY SCARVES

Made in the USA
Middletown, DE
24 September 2020